# Soccer Drills:

## A Step-by-Step Guide on How to Coach the Perfect Practice

Dylan Joseph

Soccer Drills:
A Step-by-Step Guide on How to Coach the Perfect Practice
By: Dylan Joseph
© 2020

# WAIT!

Wouldn't it be nice to have an easy two-page FREE PDF printout with two already-made practice plans? Well, here is your chance!

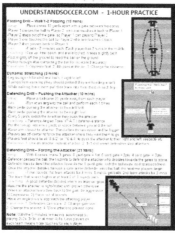

Go to this Link for an **Instant** Two-Page Printout:
UnderstandSoccer.com/free-printout

These two FREE practice plans are simply a thank you for purchasing this book. These PDF printouts will ensure that you have terrific practices for your soccer team!

# Table of Contents

# *Dedication*

This book is dedicated to you, the soccer coach, who cares about improving your players and improving yourself in the process. Learning to help others is exceptionally noble and speaks volumes about the person you are.

Also, this book is dedicated to Aaron Byrd, my soccer mentor. Working for him for over a decade at Next Level Training has allowed me to perfect many of the drills in this book and help the next generation of outstanding soccer players. Furthermore, he really helped improve my confidence, both on and off the field. For him, I am forever grateful.

# Preface

Having terrific and easy-to-understand drills for your team will help improve their skills and ultimately help your confidence as a coach. This book gives you the tips, tricks, tweaks, and techniques to help advance your team quicker than the other teams in your league while saving you time along the way. Let us understand where drills play into the bigger picture for a soccer player's development.

## INDIVIDUAL SOCCER PLAYER'S PYRAMID

If you are looking to improve your skills, your child's confidence, or your players' abilities, then it is essential to understand where this book fits into the bigger picture of developing a soccer player. In the image, the most critical field-specific skills to work on are at the base of the Individual Soccer Player's Pyramid. This pyramid is a quality outline to improve an individual soccer player's game. All the elements in the pyramid, and the items surrounding it, play a meaningful part in becoming a better player, but certain skills should be read and mastered first before moving on to the others.

You will notice that passing and receiving is at the foundation of the pyramid. This is because if you can receive and make a pass in soccer, then you will be a useful teammate. Even though you may not consistently score, dispossess the other team, or dribble through several opponents, you will still have the fundamental tools needed to play the sport and contribute to your team.

As you move one layer up, you find yourself with a decision to make on how to progress. Specifically, the pyramid is created with you in mind because each soccer player and each soccer position have different needs. Therefore, your choice regarding which path to take first is dictated by the position you play and more importantly, by the position that you want to play. In soccer and life, just because you are in a particular spot, position, or even a job, it does not mean that you must stay there forever if that is not your choice. However, it is not recommended to refuse playing a position if you are not in the exact role you want. It takes time to develop the skills that will allow you to make a shift from one position to another.

If you want to become a forward, then consider starting your route on the second layer of the pyramid with shooting and finishing. As your abilities to shoot increase, your coach will notice your new finishing skills and will be more likely to move you up the field (if you are not a forward already). Be sure to communicate to the coach that you desire to be moved up the field to a more offensive position, which will increase your chances, as well. If you are already a forward, then dive deep into this topic to ensure you become the leading scorer; first on your team, and then in the entire league. Notice that shooting and finishing is considered less critical than passing and receiving. This is because you must pass the ball up the field before you can take a shot on net.

Otherwise, you can start by progressing to dribbling and foot skills from passing and receiving because the proper technique is crucial to dribble the ball well. It is often necessary for a soccer player to use a skill to protect the ball from the other team or to advance the ball up the field to place their team in a favorable situation to score. The selection of this route is often taken first by midfielders and occasionally by forwards.

Defending is another option to proceed from passing and receiving. Keeping the other team off the scoreboard is not an easy task. Developing a defender's mindset, learning which way to push a forward, understanding how to position your body, knowing when to foul, and using the correct form for headers is critical to a defender on the back line who wants to prevent goals.

Finish all three areas in the second layer of the pyramid before progressing up the pyramid. Dribbling and defending the ball (not just shooting) are useful for an attacker; shooting and defending (not just dribbling) are helpful for a midfielder, while shooting and dribbling (not just defending) are helpful for a defender. Having a well-rounded knowledge of the skills needed for the different positions is important for all soccer players. It is especially essential for those soccer players who are looking to change positions in the future. Shooting and finishing, dribbling and foot skills, as well as defending are often more beneficial for soccer players to learn first, so focus on these before spending time on the upper areas of the pyramid. In addition, reading about each of these areas will help you understand what your opponent wants to do.

Once you have improved your skills in the first and second tiers of the pyramid, you can move up to fitness. It is difficult to go through a passing/dribbling/finishing drill for a few minutes without being out of breath. However, as you practice everything below the fitness category in the pyramid, your fitness and strength will naturally increase. Performing technical drills allows soccer players to increase their fitness naturally. This reduces the need to focus exclusively on running for fitness.

Coming from the perspective of both a soccer player and trainer, I know that constantly focusing on running is not as fulfilling and does not create long-lasting improvements, whereas emphasizing shooting capabilities, foot skills, and defending knowledge creates long-lasting change. Often, coaches who focus on running their players in practice are also coaches who want to improve their team but have limited knowledge of many of the soccer-specific topics that would quickly increase their players' abilities. Not only does fitness in soccer include your endurance; it also addresses your ability to run with agility and speed and to develop strength and power, while using stretching to improve your flexibility. All these tools put together leads to a well-rounded soccer player.

Similar to the tier below it, you should focus on the fitness areas that will help you specifically, while keeping all the topics in mind. For example, you may be a smaller soccer player who wants to put on some muscle mass. In this case, you should emphasize weight training so that you can gain the muscle needed to avoid being pushed off the ball. However, you should still stretch before and after a lifting workout or soccer practice/game to ensure that you are limber and flexible enough to recover quickly and avoid injuries.

Maybe you are a soccer player in your 20s, 30s, or 40s. Then, emphasizing your flexibility and practicing a bit of yoga would do a world of good to ensure you keep playing soccer for many more years. However, doing a few sets of push-ups, pull-ups, squats, lunges, sit-ups, etc. per week will help you maintain or gain a desirable physique.

Furthermore, you could be in the prime of your career in high school, college, or at the pro level, which means that obtaining the speed and endurance needed to run for 90+ minutes is the most essential key to continue pursuing your soccer aspirations.

Finally, we travel to the top of the pyramid, which involves tryouts. Although tryouts occur only 1-2 times per year, they have a huge impact on whether you will make the team or get left out of the lineup. Tryouts can cause intense anxiety if you do not know the keys to make sure that you stand out from your competitors and are very confident from the start.

If you have not read the *Understand Soccer* series book, *Soccer Training*, then it is highly recommended that you do so to gain the general knowledge of crucial topics within all the areas of the pyramid. Picking up a copy of the book will act as a good gauge to see how much you know about each topic, which will then help determine if a book that was later in the series written about a specific subject in the soccer pyramid will be beneficial for you.

The last portion of the pyramid are the areas that surround it. Although these are not skills and topics that can be addressed by your physical abilities, they each play key roles in rounding out a complete soccer player. For example, having one or more supportive parent(s)/guardian(s) is beneficial, as they can transport the child to games, and provide the needed equipment and the fees for the team and individual training, as well as encouragement. It is also very helpful to have a quality coach whose teachings and drills will help the individual learn how their performance and skills fit into the team's big picture.

Sleeping enough is critical to having enough energy during practices and on game days, in addition to recovering from training and games. Appropriate soccer nutrition will increase a soccer player's energy and endurance, help them achieve the ideal physique, and significantly aid in their recovery.

Understanding soccer positions will help you determine if a specific role is well-suited for your skills. It is important to know there are additional types of specific positions, not just forwards, midfielders, and defenders. A former or current professional player in the same position as you can provide guidance on the requirements to effectively play that position.

Finally, you must develop a mindset that will leave you unshakable. This mindset will help you prepare for game situations, learn how to deal with other players, and be mentally tough enough to not worry about circumstances that you cannot control, such as the type of field you play on, the officiating, or the weather.

The pyramid is a great visual aid to consider when choosing what areas to focus on next as a soccer player, coach, or parent. However, remember that a team's pyramid may look slightly different based on which tactics the players can handle and which approach the coach decides to use for games. Now that you know where this book plays into the bigger picture, let us begin.

Remember that if there are any words or terms whose meaning you are unsure of; you can feel free to reference the glossary at the back of the book.

**Finally, if you enjoy this book, please leave a review on Amazon to let me know.**

# Introduction

The overarching aim of this book is to coaches effectively plan their practices and save time. This book details various ideas on how effective practices should run, ways to motivate players, and many drills to improve your players' skills.

This book does not cover every technical aspect of soccer, such as the form for different shots, exactly how to perform the "Big 3" foot skills, or how a defender should act based on what the attacking player is doing. However, other books in the Understand Soccer series do cover those subjects and are available on Amazon.com.

The format of the book is assembled into the following sections:

1. Theory of Running a Great Practice

2. Passing & Receiving Drills

3. Dribbling & Foot Skills Drills

4. Defending Drills

5. Shooting & Finishing Drills

6. Games

# Section One:
# Theory of Running a Great Practice

# Chapter 1

## Practice Plans

As a coach who is looking for drills, and who wants to have great practices, it is important to get the most out of your players given the limited time you have to help develop their skills. This concept is often called the "Pareto Principle" or the "80/20 Rule," meaning that 80% of your team's results come from only 20% of the things your team has worked on.

The 80/20 Rule is applied throughout this book, but especially in this chapter on several strategic ways to run a practice. Therefore, you should use the following tips in practices to boost your players' skills and improve how the players' parents perceive your coaching abilities:

1. Plan your practices.
2. Have as many players as possible with a ball.
3. Favor passing drills.
4. Explain only the basics before the first lap.
5. Have as many kids moving at one time.

First, given that you have purchased and are reading a book about soccer drills, it is safe to assume you are willing to put the time in to making sure your practices are good. This is awesome and places you far ahead of most coaches who "shoot from the hip" and make it up as they go. Similar to how you spend time learning drills to use with your team in practice, make sure you spend time to plan each practice as well. **Spending 10 minutes prior to practice** to determine a practice plan will reduce any stress of worrying what you should teach your team, it will ensure what you teach them aligns with developing your players' strengths and mitigating their weaknesses, and it will allow you to receive much more enjoyment from the practices because you can immerse yourself in teaching the players without having to figure out what to teach them next. I have tried both "shooting from the hip" and planning sessions. Planning sessions always leads to better results for the players and more enjoyment for me because I am not stressing about what to teach next.

Now, it is important to be flexible with your practice plans, because often players will show up late or not at all, players may forget to bring their soccer ball, or there may be other unforeseen circumstances. **Therefore, for a one-hour practice, I will often plan four drills, knowing that I will only have time for three, since I usually like to include 10 minutes of small-sided scrimmages at the end. For a 90-minute practice, I will usually plan six drills, but only use four or five of them, and I will have 15 minutes of small-sided scrimmages at the end.** Remember, even if you did not get to do a drill that was in your practice plan, you can still add it to your practice plan for your team's next practice.

Second, as a rule of thumb, **run your practices in a way that allows as many of your players to have soccer balls at their feet. Practice should not just be about scrimmaging.** When I played high school soccer, we had some of the best soccer players in the state, but our school often usually never went very far in the state tournament because most of our practices revolved around: an unorganized jog that was less than a mile and took 20 minutes to run; followed by a single drill that was often focused around our 6'7" defender, working on his ability to head the ball; and finally, an 11v11 scrimmage for roughly 45 minutes. As you can see, this practice template had a lot of room for improvement and helps explain why we had a tough time performing against the top in-state competition. Therefore, you should consider limiting your scrimmages to 10 minutes at the end of a one-hour practice, or 15 minutes at the end of a 90-minute practice.

**Additionally, use small-sided scrimmages instead of full-field scrimmages, in most instances.** Let us take a high school team with 24 players as an example. Will playing 11v11 with two players sitting help the players practice and build their skills or would setting up four smaller fields where teams played 3v3 help your players' skills more? In an 11v11 scrimmage, only one player has the ball at any given time, whereas with four small-sided games, four players will build their skill with the soccer ball in a game-like situation. That is four times more players obtaining experience with a ball at their feet than with a full field 11v11 scrimmage.

Furthermore, setting up six small fields to play 2v2 would work wonderfully, and there would be six players at any one time working on their skills and confidence with the ball. However, because most of an 11v11 game is played without a ball at your players' feet, it is crucial that they also work on their positioning. Therefore, the occasionally practice/scrimmage involving an 11v11 is okay too.

**Third, favor passing and receiving drills over foot skills and shooting drills.** Since passing and receiving is at the base of the Individual Soccer Player's Pyramid, it should be the foundation of any team, so work passing and receiving drills frequently. Understand that your players will generally prefer shooting drills and scrimmaging but working on passing and receiving will produce better results for your team. In fact, while practicing shooting and finishing skills, as well as dribbling and foot skills, you can often add in some passing and receiving elements because, as mentioned in the introduction to this chapter, 80% of your team's results will come from 20% of what you work on with them, and a big part of that 20% is related to passing and receiving. If your players can possess the ball effectively, then they will be tough to beat.

A trick is to incorporate shooting at the end of a passing and dribbling sequence, so it will feel like a shooting drill to your player, but you should coach and emphasize the passing portions too. If your players cannot pass or dribble, then they will generally never travel to the goal to shoot, no matter how good at shooting they are.

**Furthermore, in most instances, you should avoid emphasizing fitness during practice with no specific soccer impact.** Running can be easily assigned to players when they are away from the field. For example, running laps is often not as effective to improve your player's performance on the field as doing a passing/dribbling/shooting drill, which involves changing speed and direction, body control, and soccer-specific skill development. Additionally, defending drills are great if your team's defense needs work or if your team often has limited possession in a game and needs more training on how to win the ball and prevent the other team from scoring.

**Fourth, when your players are getting water, use that time to set up the next drill.** Then, prior to their first few laps, explain only the essentials of what they need to do, often without explaining the "why." Then, for example, say you are doing a drill with four sets of four laps. Use the time during the drill to add coaching points.

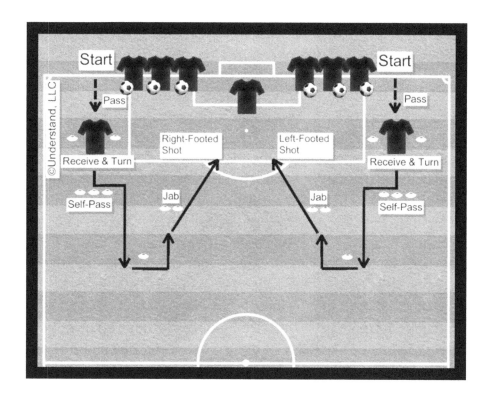

One of my favorite ways to help players grow is to stand at each set of cones in the drill to provide real-time feedback. Using the drill in the image as an example, for the first set of four laps, stand at the "Receive & Turn" portion of the drill and provide feedback. Then, during the second set of four laps, stand at the "Self-Pass" portion to ensure that the players' self-passes are done flawlessly. During the third set of four laps, stand at the "Jab" portion to make sure your players' form is on point. Finally, during the fourth lap, you can observe your players' shooting form, while providing positive feedback on the correct parts of their form and helping them with the portions of their form that have room for improvement. Too many coaches only provide feedback between sets. However, providing feedback immediately after a player does something right or wrong will ensure that it sticks with them longer than it would if you waited until after four laps of the drill were completed, and several minutes had gone by.

   **Use the time in between sets, when your players are catching their breath, to explain the "why" during the drill.** Explain why they should use a jab step/body feint when a defender is backpedaling versus a self-pass when the defender is reaching in. Show the various ways to receive a pass and turn with the ball. Teach the reasons why your players should demand and yell for the ball when receiving any passes in a drill to ensure it carries over to the field. Teaching in this fashion gives you much more time to teach your players throughout the drill than the coach who wants to explain everything at the beginning of the four sets of four laps and provides little coaching thereafter. (Note: Depending on the age of your players and the complexity of the drill, consider having one "jog-through" lap before your four sets of four laps as a way for players to ask more questions, and make sure everyone understands what must be done in the drill.)

   Fifth, you should have as many players moving at once during a drill. Most coaches will start a drill with everyone at the first cone. However, just as you should have as many players with a ball at their feet as possible during practice, you should also **have a few players start at different spots in the drill.**

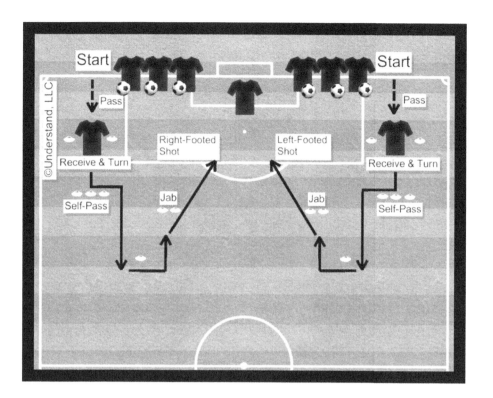

For example, as shown in the image, two starting lines is better than only one. Also, most coaches will place a player at each "Pass & Turn" portion of the drill, and the rest of the players in the two starting lines. Instead, start players with soccer balls at the cones closest to the halfway line, and their first move in the drill will be attacking the two cones to perform a jab step/body feint. This small trick will allow more players to work at any given time, and from the parents' point-of-view, more players will appear to be moving and improving their skills. **Since perception is often reality for many people, how your players' parents perceive your coaching abilities will determine whether they like you as their child's coach.** Although this is not always the most fun thing to think about, when the parents see more players being active and moving at any given time, they will perceive their kids obtaining a "good workout," which will improve their perception of you, as well.

Here is a summary of the tips to take away:

1. **Take 10 minutes to plan your practice.** Ensure that as many players have the ball at their feet as possible to boost their skills and confidence with the ball. Although there is very little idle standing during my drills and practices, I will tell my players that if they ever have a few seconds in which they are standing with a ball, and I am not talking/teaching, then they should juggle the ball to help get a feel for and control over the ball.

2. **A good portion of your practice should involve passing and receiving drills.** Explain only the essentials of a drill prior to the players' first lap. Provide immediate feedback during the drill and coaching tips between sets. Explain why they are doing the drill after they have done a few practice laps.

3. **Have as many players moving** during the drill as possible, so there will be less standing around, physical abilities and soccer skills will improve faster, and the parents' perception of your coaching abilities will increase.

# Chapter 2

## The Ajax Training Method

This chapter was adapted from the *Understand Soccer* series book, *Soccer Coaching*. Apply these principles to your team's drills to ensure that they are focusing on the most relevant skills for their age group.

In international club soccer, the biggest non-national teams play each other over the course of a season and in tournaments to determine the best teams in the world. Some examples of club teams are: Real Madrid, Paris Saint-Germain, Manchester United, Juventus, River Plate, and Bayern Munich.

**Clubs have two traditional ways of obtaining good players.** The clubs listed in the previous paragraph tend to purchase their players for large sums of money. The other type of club takes young talent and trains them to become one of the world's top performers. Often, the trained players become so good that the club sells them for large sums of money to teams willing to pay. One of the best examples of a club falling into the latter category is Ajax, a team from the Netherlands. This club is constantly advancing in international competitions because of their educational programs for their young athletes, and not because of purchasing superstar players. This speaks volumes to their training methodologies. A few of the top names to come from within their ranks and have trained from a young age are Johan Cruyff, Christian Eriksen, Wesley Sneijder, and Dennis Bergkamp. Zlatan Ibrahimović and Luis Suárez also played for Ajax too.

One of the biggest underlying decisions impacting their training is the focus on age-specific soccer skills. Players 12 years old and younger focus mostly on technique with the ball. This means they are working on their ability to shoot and finish, pass and receive with proper form, heading the ball, learning the various foot skills and best forms of dribbling. The logic behind this is that these players will play in many systems over the course of their career. Therefore, it is best to focus on building the player, so they can easily adapt to any coaching system. This style of training ensures they are taking more touches with the ball than nearly all the other players their age. More deliberate touches will quickly raise their confidence and ability to be an effective soccer player who can play on the game's biggest stages.

Next, between the ages of 12-15 years old, players' attention should be directed towards working as a team and becoming comfortable with building a play by passing the ball. Granted, this does not mean that players who are 12 years old or younger players should never pass the ball, nor does it mean that players who are 12-15-years old should never focus on shooting and foot skills; it is merely pointing out what the main emphasis of the practice should be during these ages.

Then players who are 15+ years old will change their focus to the tactical progression of a team's play style. This age group will focus on where each player fits into the team's overarching theme. Ajax has found this to be an appropriate time to increase their strength training, as well.

This is a sound system for a club. Granted, you may be the coach of only one age group. However, prioritizing certain types of training over different periods of a soccer player's career with your club will turn it into a premier organization with players who are excited to join. Yes, this will take coordination with club directors and other coaches, but it is worth it.

Remember that it makes little sense to focus only on foot skills with 18-year-olds and focus only on team tactics with eight-year-olds. Therefore, the training that will be appropriate for each player will be highly dependent on their age.

# Chapter 3

## Motivating Players

In an ideal world, you would not need to motivate players at all. They would all arrive at practice five minutes early, always smiling, and they would do everything you say. Sadly, you will often find that, while most of the players on your team are self-motivated, a few will seem indifferent, and one or two players will need all the motivation and help you can give them. The Athletic Footwear Association survey of 20,000+ young soccer players found that children want to play soccer for the following reasons, listed in order of importance:

1. Have fun.

2. Improve their skills.

3. Stay in shape.

4. Do something they are good at.

5. Excitement of competition.

6. Exercise.

7. Play as part of a team.

8. Challenge of competition.

9. Learn new skills.

10. Win matches.

Therefore, use this list as a general guideline to determine what drives your players and to understand what needs are most important to meet for your players to help them feel motivated. Now, remember that those polled were young players, so it is safe to assume if you have older players (i.e., teenagers, college players, or pros) the order can change. Since this list comprises the things your players want from soccer, let us discuss how you can help meet their needs to increase their motivation.

Though having pre-planned sessions was a topic already discussed a bit in the first chapter, **disorganized training sessions can be demotivating to soccer players because a significant portion of the practice feels like wasted time.** Also, a disorganized practice often does not meaningfully improve a players' skills. Plan drills that follow the three C's:

**1. Competitive**: Many of the drills in this book can be a competition between groups, an individual against oneself, or a team competition against the clock.

**2. Challenging**: Generally, your players should be sweaty after they are done practicing. This will ensure that they worked hard during your session.

**3. Capable**: Create training sessions that will make your players feel capable of learning the skills and understanding the drills within a reasonable period. For example, teaching the bicycle/overhead kick to a group of six-year-olds is unreasonable.

Additionally, young players often are not good at assessing their own skills, so they rely on coaches, parents, and teammates to tell them how they are doing. Given that you are their coach, they are most likely to listen to you. If you have feedback which will significantly improve their game, then consider using the "sandwich technique" previously mentioned in the first book of the *Understand Soccer* series, *Soccer Training*.

**To use the sandwich technique when giving feedback,** first, give a compliment on something they are performing well. Keep the praise quick and straightforward, such as, "Good job approaching the ball diagonally when shooting." Then, give feedback and explain why. For example, say, "Plant your foot farther from the ball which will allow you to turn your toe down and out more." Finally, end with another compliment and explanation like, "Great job following through; you are good at that."

Although children have different personalities, the sandwich method is great, both for players who are open to feedback and players who have a fixed mindset. By beginning with a compliment, you will break down any walls that they may have built up against feedback. By ending with a compliment, you will leave them with the good feeling that they are doing most things correctly. **By providing constructive feedback in the middle of two compliments, you will make sure that they hear your message, but they will also have positive associations with it.** The two compliments will also act as positive reinforcement, so they will continue to do the things you praised them for successfully doing.

Similar to giving your players feedback, be open to feedback as well. Do not be afraid to ask questions. (E.g., on a scale of 1 to 10, how much did you like that drill? How fun was practice? What was your favorite thing you learned today?) Showing your openness to improving will go a long way with the players and parents too.

**Next, the most demotivating thing for a player is not playing.** Although this is a tougher subject for high school and college coaches, not playing someone will probably wreck their mindset in the short-term and make them less likely to work harder during practice because they will feel that it will not result in playing time anyway. Ideally, a player will have the mindset of, "Well, if I am not playing, then I need to work even harder, so I can play." This mindset will help a player go a lot farther than most other players who lack this mindset. However, please understand that only about one out of every 10 or so players will think that way. Therefore, most players do not just want to sit on the bench, while they watch all their teammates have fun. They want to be a part of the game, too.

Now, it is not suggested that every player should have equal playing time, nor is it suggested that you should give every player playing time if your main aim is to win right now. However, you should give some play time to the players on your team if you are looking to have every player motivated on your team. Also, make sure you are up front with players and parents if there is a chance some players receive little or no playing time. **90% of young soccer players polled revealed they would rather be on a losing team and play rather than be on a winning team and sit on the bench.** If there is a player(s) that you will likely be benching for most of the season and want to keep their spirits up as best you can, make sure to constantly discuss the "team first" mentality with them.

**Lastly, great body language as a coach is important. Be approachable by smiling, be quick to laugh with players, and do not cross your arms in front of you or behind you.** Whether crossed in front of your body, behind your body, or resting tightly by your sides, you are sending the message, "I am unapproachable, I am nervous, I am awkward, I am mean, and you should not talk to me." Loosen up your arms, bend at the elbows, and relax. If you use your hands while talking, great; just avoid being too rigid. Though scare tactics can work in the short term, they hardly lead to long-term success. Over the course of an entire season, playing for the "mean coach" often is very demotivating.

In conclusion, be sure to do your part by adding to your players' motivation. Here is a summary of the tips to takeaway:

1. Have well-planned training sessions.

2. Give feedback.

3. Play your players.

4. Be approachable.

# Chapter 4

# 5 Topics Every Coach Should Teach in Practice

1. **Anticipate, do not react.** Renato Susnja, former Division 1 college midfielder and an outstanding soccer trainer at Next Level Training, often says that it is important to **"anticipate, do not react."** This attitude will allow players to imagine what will happen *before* it happens. When players use in-game visualization, such as expecting a play to happen, they will be afforded the time they need to make an action plan. I have had several coaches and players ask me, "What is the most important thing I can implement for myself or my players to become better immediately?" I respond with two things: (1) Take a moving first touch; and (2) Constantly ask, "If I received the ball right now, what would I do with it?" Therefore, as a coach who is looking to help your players make faster in-game decisions, the trick is to decide what they are going to do with the ball before they receive it. This is a great tip to give your players prior to scrimmaging at the end of your practice.

So many soccer players, myself included for many years, would watch and wait to receive the soccer ball and once I finally received a pass, I would then need to figure out what I needed to do with the ball. The problem was this resulted in a lot of settling touches underneath my body which made it extremely easy for the other team to apply pressure and poke the ball away. This destroyed my confidence because I never felt like I had enough time to do something with the ball. Instead, teach your players to ask themselves constantly, "What would I do if I received the ball right now?"

This one question alone makes players more likely to scan the field to help decide what to do next, it allows players to also consider what they would need to do in order to get open to receive a pass, and it also helps prevent younger players from playing "herd soccer" where most of the players are bunched up in the middle of the field. Also, because the player will have decided what to do with the ball before they received it, they will have visualized what should be done in their mind. When they receive the ball, they will be more successful because they will have already done it once in their mind, and now they will do it a second time, but this time in reality. Lastly, by having a plan before they receive the ball, it makes it easier to take a moving first touch in the direction they want to travel and will allow them to increase their speed of play, which is a struggle for most soccer players to overcome and is a difficult area for most coaches to help their players improve.

2. **Instruct your players to avoid saying negative things out loud.** Trevor Moawad is a renowned mental conditioning expert and strategic advisor to some of the world's most elite performers. Also, he was named the "Sports World's Best Brain Trainer" by *Sports Illustrated*. He reveals that players do not want to be positive when their game is tanking (e.g., a goalkeeper who just let in two goals, or a forward who missed an empty net). Based on his research, he found that negativity is amplified through externalization. Essentially, this means that saying something out loud makes it 10X more powerful than just thinking it. Also, negativity is 4-7X more powerful than positivity.

Trevor worked with Coach Nick Saban of the University of Alabama collegiate football program, who won five national championships in a nine-year period from 2009 to 2017. To go on this historic run of championship seasons, they discovered that negativity was the most powerful element players were facing. Therefore, the goal was to get players not to say negative/destructive things out loud. In fact, they did not even teach any "positive thinking" tricks. The only thing expected of the players was that they eliminate their verbal complaining about the weather, the field condition, a coach's decision, a referees' call, how hard a drill was, and other general circumstances.

If a player says negative statements out loud, they are predicting, visualizing, and perpetuating exactly what they do not want to have happen. By you not allowing negativity to be said out loud, players will begin to stop verbalizing their negativity. Their thoughts may swirl, but they are always in control of what they say. Making mistakes hurts and the past is real, but the only thing that makes the past predictive is if your players' behavior stays the same. Behavior predicts success. By changing your players' language, you will help change their behavior positively. Even worse than a player impacting their own performance by saying negative things, what they say out loud will impact other players' mindsets and lead their teammates to have more negative thoughts too. Therefore, give this advice at the beginning of the season and make sure your players stick to it. If you adopt a mission statement for your team, this should be a part of it.

3. **Have your players ask better questions**. If your player makes a mistake and mentally asks, "Why am I so bad" or "Why do I keep messing up," they will surely be able to give answers which will not help them overcome their difficulties.

With questions like those, players will naturally answer them with statements like:

-"Because I am dumb."

-"Because I am no good."

-"Because no one believes in me."

-"Because I am lazy."


Instead, tell your players to ask better questions, like:

-"How can I avoid making this mistake again?"

-"What could I have done differently?"

-"What can I learn from this?"


These better questions help your players focus on what to improve going forward rather than mulling on their mistakes of the past. Because these are conversations that will occur in a player's head or under their breath, you will not hear them happening. Make sure you teach your players what are good questions versus which questions are bad and should be avoided, so they know how to handle the situation themselves when it arises. Similar to the second point, this is best taught at the beginning of the season and then have occasionally reminders to the entire squad when players are getting down on themselves.

4. **Your team plays how they practice**. You have likely heard this one before, but it is worth repeating. If your team has lazy practices and lackluster drills, and you do not expect too much from your players in practice, then their skills will stagnate, while the players on the other teams in the league are improving. Even the best player on your team who does not

take practices seriously will soon find the less-talented players outperforming them because of their lack of hard work and effort in practices. Make sure that your players give 100% in practice today to ensure that they will grow and give 110% in the next game.

5. **Remind your players to keep their heads up**. Whether your team has been scored on once or is down by four goals, remind your players to keep their heads held high and tell their teammates to keep their heads up, too. By ensuring that your players maintain positive body language, it will seem easier to make a comeback, and you will keep them in a more positive state of mind.

A few years ago, our team signed a new goalkeeper, Zack Raymond. Right from the first game, he started telling me to pick my head up and I was the team's striker and leading goal-scorer in previous seasons! In fact, he even yelled from the other side of the field to tell me to pick my head up. It impressed me that he was such a confident person and what he said was great advice. Even when I made a mistake—which was more often than I want to admit—Zack knew the importance of making sure that I had positive body language, both so that I would perform better, and so that the other players on the team who looked up to me would stay positive, too.

Hold your players accountable and have them remind each other to keep their heads up. Also, when you notice a head that is "down" during a game, simply yell out, "Heads up!" as a quick reminder.

# Section Two:
# Drills

# Introduction to Drills

In the following sections, each drill is set up using the same template to easily understand which drills should be used to help improve different skills on your team. Also, if a drill says it is for 4-8 players, and you have a squad of 18 players, then set up three grids of the drill, so each grid will have six players. Use your best judgment when setting up the drills and know that you can change them as you see fit, based on the amount of space you have available, the number of players at practice, how many cones you have, how much time you have, how many soccer balls are available, the skill level of your players, and whether you think something can be improved.

Each drill includes coaching points to give you additional things to teach, and information to share while working on each of the drills with your team. Should any of the drills become boring for you or your players, there are variations to perform, which will allow you to change the drill after each set or make it more difficult as your players become accustomed to the basics principles of the drill.

In all the following images, dashed lines indicate a pass, whereas solid lines indicate when a player should be dribbling the ball or running. If there are any terms you are unaware of, please reference the glossary at the back of this book.

# Passing Drills

# Chapter 6

# Passing Drill 1—Wall Passes (1-2 Passing)

**# of Players Needed:** 3

**Purpose:**

-A wall pass is when you pass the ball to a teammate, and they pass it back to you with one touch.

-One-touch passing speeds the pace of play.

-Also, it reduces the time your opponents have to react and defend.

**Setup:**

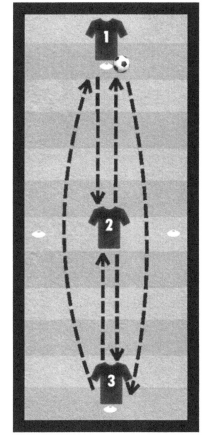

1. Set up two cones 10 yards apart, then set up a gate by placing another two cones halfway between the cones that are 10 yards apart.

2. Have one player stand at each outside cone and one player at the middle gate.

3. Player 1 starts with the ball. They pass the ball five yards to Player 2, who one-touches it back to Player 1.

4. Player 2 steps out of the gate, so Player 1 can send a 10-yard pass to Player 3.

5. Player 3 one-touches the ball to Player 2, who one-touches it back to Player 3.

6. Player 3 then sends a 10-yard pass back to Player 1.

**Sets:**

-Perform 6 sets that are 2 minutes each.

-Each player takes 2 turns in the middle.

**Coaching Points:**

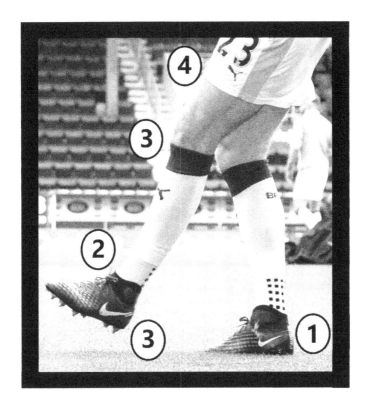

Teach this passing form to your players to make an accurate pass:

1. Plant next to the ball, while pointing your foot and hips at your teammate.

2. Keep your toes up, your heel down, and your ankle locked.

3. Keep your knees slightly bent and your foot slightly off the ground.

4. Follow through after making contact with the ball.

**Variations:**

-Have your players use their opposite foot.

-Instruct every 4<sup>th</sup> pass to be played in the air. This will help your players work on playing one-touch passes from passes received in the air. Also, it will work on their mental focus by forcing them to keep track of whether the next pass should be on the ground or in the air.

-Add more distance between the cones.

     **YouTube:** If you would like to see a video on this passing drill, then consider watching the *Understand Soccer* YouTube video: *Wall Passing Drills*.

# Chapter 7

## Passing Drill 2—Rondo

**# of Players Needed:** 4 or more

**Purpose:**

-A Rondo is a training game similar to "keep away" where one group of players must maintain possession of the ball by passing it around members of the opposing side.

-Rondos teach your team how to work together, pass in tight spaces, avoid holding onto the ball for too long, and how to make decisions quickly.

**Setup:**

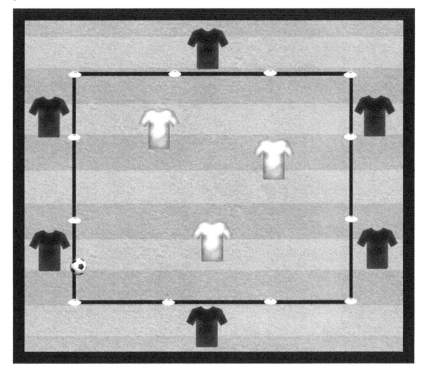

1. Set up a 15-yard x 15-yard box.

2. Have six players on the outside, and three players on the inside.

3. When the players in the middle obtain possession of the ball, have the person who made the mistake (and the players to their right and left) enter the inside of the square.

4. Then have the three players that were inside the square switch to the outside.

**Sets:**

-Have your players perform this for 15 minutes.

-Do not give breaks to help simulate a game and because being on the outside is not very tiring.

**Coaching Points:**

1. Emphasize creating triangle shapes and teaching your players how to move so the player passing the ball always has two teammates open as targets.

2. Teach transitioning from offense to defense when possession is lost by initially allowing the players on the inside to walk to their positions on the outside of the square. Then, to simulate a more game-like approach, direct players to immediately transition when possession changes. Immediately transitioning when possession changes forces players to develop their transitional awareness and mindset to keep them from being caught off guard.

3. Having a complex Rondo or one where the players must play one-touch will not be very helpful for a team of 7-year-olds.

Conversely, allowing many touches in a huge space will not make high school soccer players much better.

**Variations:**

-Decrease the size of the square as your players become more comfortable with rondos as the season progresses.

-Limit their number of touches to 2 or 1 to improve their skills related to passing and receiving.

# Chapter 8

# Passing Drill 3—Increasing Distance Passing

**# of Players Needed:** 10 or more

**Purpose:**

-To work on two-and-one-touch passing at increasing distances.

-To develop an attacking first touch.

-To increase communication.

-To focus on leading passes.

**Setup:**

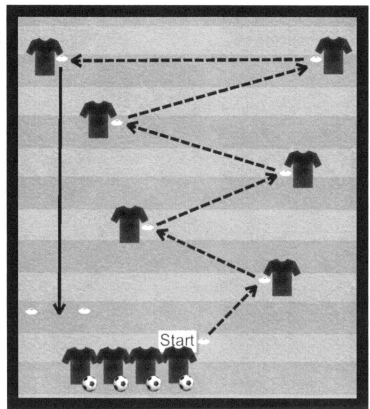

1. Set up each cone a little farther away than the previous one.

2. Set up the first cone about three yards diagonal to the "Start." Also, consider placing a cone at the "Start," so your players will know where to line up.

3. Set up the second cone five yards diagonal to the "Start."

4. Set up the third, fourth, fifth, and sixth cones seven, 10, 13, and 16 yards away, respectively.

5. Set up a gate of two cones about 18 yards away from the sixth cone.

6. Have one player start at each cone, and at least four players with soccer balls at the "Start."

7. Have the first player at the "Start" play the ball to the player at Cone 1.

8. Once the player at Cone 1 receives the pass from Player 1, they will turn and play the ball to the player at Cone 2. Continue in this manner for the player at each cone.

9. Player 1 will follow their pass to the cone, then the second player at the "Start" will step up and pass them the ball. Continue in this manner for all players at the "Start."

10. When the player at Cone 6 receives their pass, their aim is to take one moving first touch of the ball through the gate, and then return to the "Start."

**Sets:**

-3-4 sets, with 3-4 laps per set

**Coaching Points:**

1. Ensure each player is demanding the ball. (Focusing on communicating in practice ensures your players are more likely to do it during a game with no need to think about it.)

2. Make sure players are actively on their toes to react quickly for good or bad passes.

-Emphasize proper passing form: 1) Toe Up 2) Heal Down 3) Ankle Locked 4) Knee Slightly Bent 5) Foot Slightly Off the Ground.

3. Player passing to their right (Cones 1, 3, & 5) should pass with their right foot.

4. Player passing to their left (Cones 2 & 4) should pass with their left foot.

5. The player at cone 6 is travelling to their right, so they should take a moving first touch with their right foot.

6. They are allowed one touch to travel through the 1-yard wide gate.

**Variations:**

-You can make it a team competition by counting the total number of times players one-touch the ball through the gate. After their first set of counting their total team score, teach them to lead teammates with their passes because it can make a 15-yard touch a lot easier by having to only push it 7-8 yards if the ball is played properly in front of the player. Also, the player will have already generated speed when they take their first touch.

-Depending on the age of your players, you can start them at two touch passing. As they become comfortable with the drill, require they only do one touch passing.

-This drill can be easily reversed to have more touches with your players left foot than their right to focus on the opposite foot.

# Chapter 9

## Passing Drill 4—Long-Short-Short

**# of Players Needed:** 3-4 per group

**Purpose:**

-To develop skills when playing and receiving passes.

-To teach players how to follow their pass and ensure that in a game, the player receiving the pass has an option for someone to pass the ball to.

-To work on one-and-two-touch passing.

**Setup:**

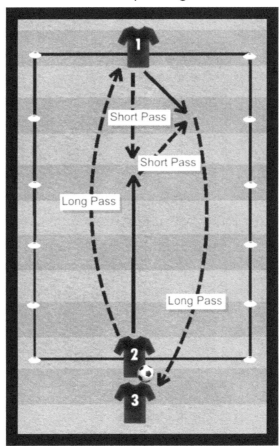

1. Start with 3-4 players in two lines 30 yards apart.

2. Player 2 will chip the ball to Player 1, and then run directly at Player 1.

3. Player 1 will settle the ball, and then pass it back to Player 2.

4. Player 2 will softly one-touch the ball to the side, so Player 1 can chip the ball to Player 3.

5. Player 1 will sprint toward Player 3.

6. Player 3 will settle the ball, and then pass it back to Player 1.

7. Player 1 will lay the ball to the side, so Player 3 can chip the ball to Player 2.

8. Player 3 will sprint to Player 2.

9. Repeat.

## Sets:

-Perform 4 sets for 4 minutes each.

-Have 1 minute of rest between sets to allow for time to tell players what they are doing well and where they can improve.

## Coaching Points:

1. Tell the players to keep their heads down when chipping the ball to keep their form together for a more accurate chip.

2. Emphasize the passing and receiving form: 1) toe up 2) heal down 3) ankle locked 4) knee bent 5) foot slightly off the ground.

3. Have players constantly demanding the ball and yelling for the pass.

**Variations:**

-Reverse the lay-off. So, instead of passing the ball to the right, the player who made the long pass will lay the next pass to their left.

-Instead of lofting the ball for the initial pass, have the player drive the ball a few feet off the ground or keep the ball on the ground the entire time.

-Instead of the player receiving the lofted pass using two touches, have them pass the ball back with only one touch.

# Dribbling Drills

# Chapter 10

# Dribbling Drill 1—Fast Footwork

**# of Players Needed:** 1-100+

**Purpose:**

-Acts as a great first drill of practice to warm up your players.

-Easy for you to assess a player's technical dribbling and foot skill abilities when first working with them.

-Allows your players a ton of touches in a short time. This drill and concept of more touches in less time is discussed in great length in the *Understand Soccer* series book, *Soccer Dribbling & Foot Skills*.

**Setup:**

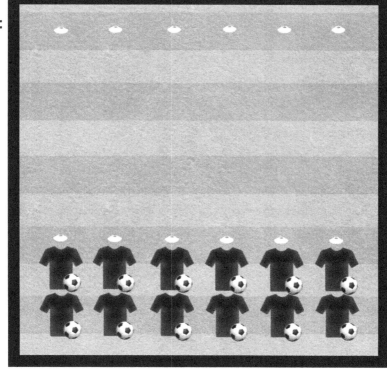

1. Set up two cones on the field about 15-20 yards away from each other. Fast footwork will be practiced by working from one cone to the other and then back.

2. Set up cones 15-20 yards away from each player on your team. If you do not have enough cones or space, then break the team up into groups of two or three.

**Sets:**

1. Small Dribbles

2. Speed Dribbles

3. Out-and-Ins

4. Push Stop

5. Self-Passes

6. Roll Touch

7. Rolls

8. Roll Stop

9. Step-On-Step-Outs

10. Touch Scissor

**Coaching Points:**

1. **Small Dribbles** – With your toes pointed down and in, push the ball forward with the bone of your foot. Go for as many touches as possible from one cone to the other. Then, switch feet and repeat.

2. **Speed Dribbles** – With your toes pointed down and in, push the ball forward with the bone of your foot. Go for a touch every single step from one cone to the other. Then, switch feet and repeat.

3. **Out-and-Ins** – With your toes pointed down and in, push the ball diagonal with the bone of your foot (out). Then, cut the ball with the inside of your foot (in). Go for as many touches as possible from one cone to the other. Then, switch feet and repeat.

4. **Push Stop** – With your toes pointed down and in, push the ball forward with the bone of your foot. Then, stop the ball with the bottom of the same foot that pushed it. Then, immediately switch feet and repeat.

5. **Self-Passes** – Using both feet, perform a pass from one foot to the other. Then, push the ball forward with the inside of the foot that received the pass. Using the same foot that pushed the ball, pass the ball back across your body, so you can push the ball forward with the other foot.

6. **Roll Touch** – Facing forward, roll the ball across your body. Then take a touch-up with the opposite foot. Switch feet and roll the ball back across your body, then push the ball up with the opposite foot.

7. **Rolls** – With your body turned to the right, and the side of your shoulder pointed towards the opposite cone, roll the ball using the bottom of your foot. Repeat with the opposite foot. Remember, when rolling the ball with the bottom of your foot, always use the bottom of your toes. Using the bottom of your heel, or the bottom of your arch, will not allow you to reach as far and your foot is more likely to bounce off the ball. Also, you have the most nerve endings in your toes, which means your toes have the best feel for the ball.

8. **Roll Stop** – Similar to a roll, with your shoulders turned sideways, roll the ball with the bottom of your toes but stop the ball with the inside of your opposite foot. Then, with the foot that

rolled the ball, roll the ball again. Repeat this with your opposite foot.

9. **Step-On-Step-Outs** – With your toes pointed down and in, push the ball diagonal with the bone of your foot. Then, stop it with the bottom of your toes. Then, immediately push the ball diagonal with your opposite foot and stop it with the bottom of your toes. Then, repeat, switching back and forth, using both feet.

10. **Touch Scissor** – Using only one foot, touch the ball forward with your toes pointed down and in. Then, with the same foot, perform a scissor. Then, move the ball with the same foot and perform another scissor.

**Variation:**

-Set up a line of cones with each cone spaced one yard apart. Perform these fast footwork skills between cones to increase your player's precision and accuracy of their touch.

**YouTube:** If you would like to see a video on this dribbling drill, then consider watching the *Understand Soccer* YouTube video: *Soccer Dribbling Drills for Kids*.

# Chapter 11

## Dribbling Drill 2—Cross

**# of Players Needed:** 1-2 per grid.

**Purpose:**

-To develop confidence dribbling in tight spaces.

-To work on foot skills including the "Big 3" foot skills.

-Acts as a great warm-up/first drill.

**Setup:**

Base Cone Formation:

Foot Skills:

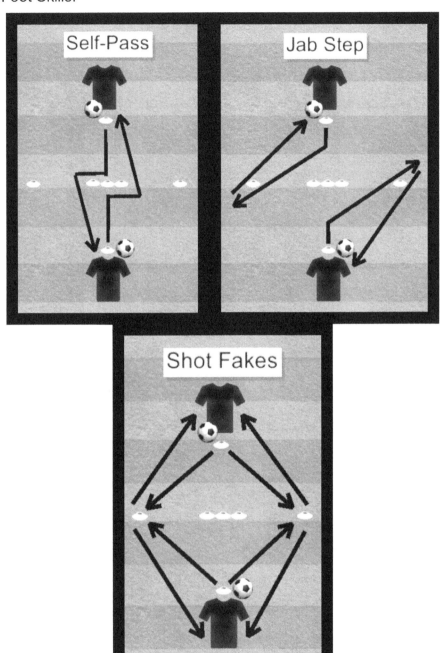

**Sets:**

-Self-Passes – Right to left.

-Self-Passes – Left to right.

-Jab Steps (Body Feints) – Left jab step, then right foot pushes.

-Jab Steps (Body Feints) – Right jab step, then left foot pushes.

-Cut, Chop, and Step-On-Step-Out Shot Fakes – Going to both the right and left in the same set and staying on their side of the cross the entire time.

**Coaching Points:**

1. Emphasize one touch in between each set of cones. Less touches are quicker.

2. Explode after doing a skill.

3. Make sure their shot fakes look like shots. Arms and leg up.

4. Do not let players skip cones. Each skipped cone is a missed rep, and they add up!

5. Works great as a first drill of practice as players show up late to just set up another few cones.

**Variations:**

-Though it is not recommended to teach lesser skills like the roll, scissor, and several of the shot fakes like the V Pull-Back and Jump Turn, they can be added if you would like to teach them.

**YouTube:** If you would like to see a video on this dribbling drill, then consider watching the *Understand Soccer* YouTube video: *Soccer Drills for Kids*.

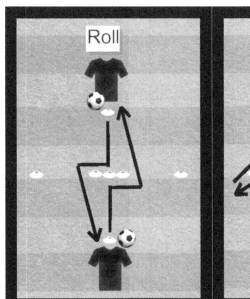

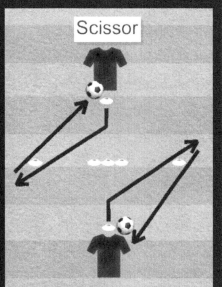

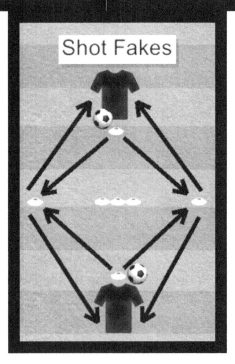

# Chapter 12

# *Dribbling Drill 3—Shot Fakes without Cones*

**# of Players Needed:** 1-100+

**Purpose:**

-To develop players' shot fakes.

-To practice players' explosiveness after a skill.

-To work on improving your players' comfort with pushing the ball without taking a touch every step.

**Setup:**

1. Use two lines on the field that are five yards apart (or the six-yard box).

2. Starting at one line, have your players push the ball to the other line with their toe down and in, using the bone of their foot, with only one touch.

3. Once at the other line, perform a right-footed shot fake.

4. Next, accelerate back to the starting line, with only one touch.

5. Then, perform a left-footed shot fake.

6. Continue to alternate between right-and-left-footed shot fakes.

**Sets:**

-Perform a set of 10 shot fakes (5 right-footed and 5 left-footed) starting with the cut shot fake. Perform 6 sets total using three different shot fakes.

-My recommendation is to do the Tier 1 shot fakes (Cut, Chop, and Step-On-Step-Out) 2X each.

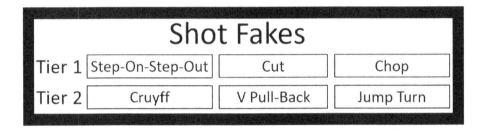

| Shot Fakes | | |
|---|---|---|
| Tier 1 | Step-On-Step-Out | Cut | Chop |
| Tier 2 | Cruyff | V Pull-Back | Jump Turn |

**Coaching Points:**

1. Make sure your players' shot fakes look like their actual shots. They need their arms up and shooting leg back at a minimum to make it believable.

2. A Step-On-Step-Out Shot Fake is great for when your player wants to continue attacking in the direction they are facing.

3. A Cut Shot Fake where the player keeps the ball in front of themselves by cutting the ball with the inside of their foot is good to use when there is plenty of space between the player using the shot fake and the defender.

4. A Chop Shot Fake where the player places themselves between the defender and the ball by cutting the ball with the outside of their foot is good to use when there is not much space between the player using the shot fake and the defender.

**Variations:**

-Perform the Tier 2 shot fakes (e.g., Jump Turn, Cruyff, and V Pull-Back).

-Travel 10 yards, instead of five yards.

# Chapter 13

## Dribbling Drill 4—"Big 3" Foot Skills

**# of Players Needed:** 2-6 per grid

**Purpose:**

-To emphasize the "Big 3" foot skills.

-To work on being explosive after performing a skill.

**Setup:**

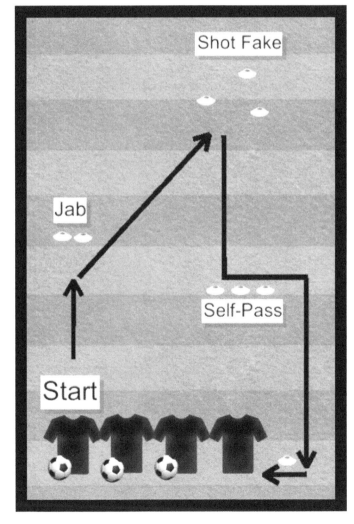

1. Attack the first two cones and perform a left-footed jab step.

2. Accelerate to the shot fake (the three cones in a triangle).

3. Perform a right-footed chop shot fake.

4. Accelerate with one push from your right foot to the three cones in a line to perform a self-pass.

5. Do a la croqueta/self-pass by passing the ball from your right foot to your left foot.

6. Accelerate to the next cone and use a right-footed chop just past the cone.

7. Finally, accelerate back to the start.

**Sets:**
-Perform six sets, with four laps per set.

**Coaching Points:**
1. Use only one push to accelerate to the next set of cones.
2. Dribble with your head slightly up, not straight down at the ball.
3. Make your shot fake look believable.

**Variations:**

-Change up the shot fakes each set. Perform chops, step-on-step-outs, and cruyffs.

-Once your players have gotten used to the drill as is, you can reverse it, so your players will use the opposite foot when performing each of the skills.

# Chapter 14

# Dribbling Drill 5—Moving First Touch & "Big 3" Foot Skills

**# of Players Needed:** 4-8

**Purpose:**

-Player receiving the pass works on yelling for the ball, attacking with the correct foot, and using one roughly 10-yard moving first touch.

-Player passing works on playing leading passes.

-To develop the "Big 3" foot skills.

**Setup:**

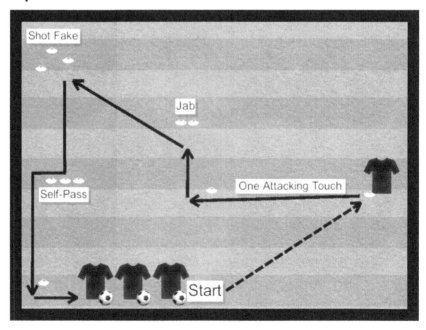

1. Set up the initial cone about 12 yards away from the "Start."

2. Set up the next cone about 10 yards away from the first cone.

3. After taking a right-footed moving first touch, cut around the cone and perform a right-footed jab step.

4. Then, push the ball diagonally to the left, while exploding after the ball.

5. Perform a left-footed shot fake at the three cones and accelerate away.

6. Then, perform a left-to-right self-pass.

7. Push the ball with one touch past the final cone.

8. Then, go back to the "Start" and repeat.

## Sets:
-Perform 4 sets with 4 laps per set.

## Coaching Points:
1. Ask the player at the "Start" not to pass the ball until the player receiving the ball yells and demands the ball.

2. There should only be one push of the ball in between each set of cones and one touch to cut the ball when needing to travel around the cones. The quickest of players should only use 10 touches from receiving the initial pass to travel back to "Start."

3. When your player performs a jab step (body feint), make sure their ball is diagonally in front of them with their ball outside their right should, so the skill looks more believable when they fake pushing it to the right.

4. The pass from the left foot to the right foot in the self-pass should be horizontal to the defender, not diagonal. A diagonal self-pass makes it much easier for the defender to steal the ball.

**Variations:**

-For the first two laps, stand at the cones that represent the jab step (body feint). As the coach, you can pretend to be a defender to make it feel more game like for your players. For the second two laps, stand at the self-pass. Reach in, and attempt to steal the ball away from each player.

-Flip the drill, so the first pass goes towards the left instead.

-Time the players' laps and make it a competition for the entire team. While they perform their first set of four laps, time them using a stopwatch. Then, require that they beat their score by 10 seconds. Remember to avoid using the stopwatch on your phone because, to an outside observer, it may appear that you are on your phone and not paying enough attention to the players.

**YouTube:** If you would like to see a video on this dribbling drill, then consider watching the *Understand Soccer* YouTube video: *Coaching Drills for Youth Soccer*.

# Defending Drills

# Chapter 15

## Defending Drill 1—Pushing the Attacker

**# of Players Needed:** 1 or more - Each player can do this with a separate cone or their own soccer ball.

**Purpose:**

-To emphasize a curved approach to the attacker to force them in the direction you want them to go.

-To work on "Patience Angled Toes" (PAT).

-To develop a player's ability to backpedal quickly, while staying in front of the attacker.

**Setup:**

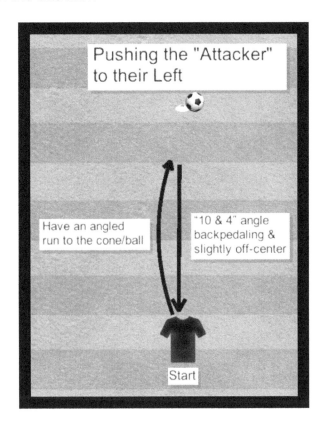

Pushing the "Attacker" to their Left

Have an angled run to the cone/ball

"10 & 4" angle backpedaling & slightly off-center

Start

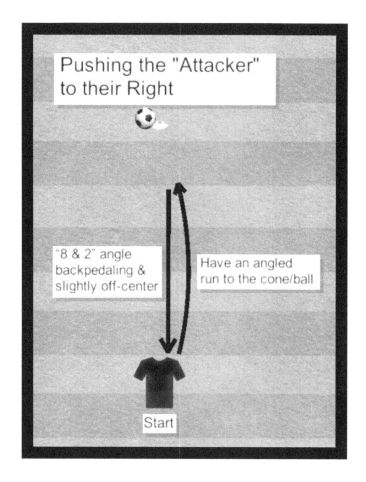

1. Place a ball or cone 25 yards away from each player. If you are limited on space, then create lines of two or three players for each ball/cone.

**Sets:**

-Perform each of the following 4 times:

-Run to a cone/ball, leaving a yard or two of space. Backpedal with an angled stance for 20 yards, pushing the attacker to their left foot.

-Run to a cone/ball, leaving a yard or two of space. Backpedal with an angled stance for 20 yards, pushing the attacker to their right foot.

-Run to a cone/ball, leaving a yard or two of space. Backpedal with an angled stance for 20 yards. Every five yards switch the direction in which the defender is pushing the attacker.

**Coaching Points:**

1. Teach the "Patience Angled Toes" (PAT) defensive stance.

2. In a game, assume the attacker is right-footed until your player observes otherwise.

3. When the attacker turns their back to the goal, be aggressive.

4. Remind your players to keep their arm closest to the attacker raised, and their elbow bent. This will make it easier to turn and will make them appear bigger.

5. Have your players run up to the ball/cone but leave a yard or two of space. This is because, in a game, if a defender runs directly at the attacker, then the attacker will dribble past the defender with ease.

6. Remember, a good defender decides where the attacker travels.

7. Ensure that your players are off-center to force the attacker in the direction you want them to travel, while keeping their feet at "8 & 2" or "10 & 4" to push the attacker to their right and left, respectively.

**Variations:**

-Have an attacker instead of a cone/ball that the defender approaches. Have the defender force the attacker in one direction as the attacker attacks with the ball.

-Eventually, have this drill turn into 1-on-1s. Award points to defenders who push the ball out-of-bounds or dispossess the attacker.

# Chapter 16

## Defending Drill 2—1v1s

**# of Players Needed:** 2-3 per grid

**Purpose:**

-To focus on the game-like situation of a 1v1.

-To work on every player's defending and attacking skills.

-To help your players work on dispossession, as well as slowing possession.

-To instruct your players how to force an attacker out-of-bounds.

-To develop your players' defensive stance.

**Setup:**

1. Set up one 10-yard-wide X 20-yard-long grid for every 2-3 players.

2. Give Player 2 and Player 3 get soccer balls to start. Player 2 attacks, while Player 1 defends.

3. The set is done when: (1) the far line is crossed by the attacking player with the ball; (2) the defender kicks the ball out-of-bounds; or (3) the defender gains possession of the ball.

4. Then, Player 1 goes back to the starting side (i.e., where Player 3 is shown in the picture). Player 2 switches from attacking Player 1 to defending against Player 3.

5. If there are players on your team who will always play defense, and others who will always attack, then certain players can always attack, and other players can always defend.

6. Try to assign the more-skilled players on your team to the same group. Assign the less-skilled players to their own group.

7. Rotate players to different groups after each set.

**Sets:**
-Perform 3 total sets with 6 minutes for each set. After 3 minutes, change the order so the person the player previously attacked against will be the person they now defend against and vice versa.

**Coaching Points:**
1. Teach your attacking players to use self-passes when the defender reaches in the for the ball.

2. Instruct the attacking players to use jab steps (body feints) when the defender is backpedaling.

3. For defenders, teach them to push the attacker to a sideline if they are close to one.

4. If the attacker is centered in the grid, then teach the defender to push the attacker to their weak foot.

5. Teach "Patience Angled Toes" (PAT) to the defenders for their defensive stance.

6. Emphasize to defenders that kicking the ball out-of-bounds can be highly effective in a game to buy your team more time to regain its defensive shape. Grab a copy of the *Understand Soccer* series book, *Soccer Defending*, to learn more about critical defensive techniques for you to teach your players.


## Variations:

-Award points: If the player attacking dribbles past the other side of the 20-yard grid, they receive a point. If the defender dispossesses the attacker, the defender gets a point. If the defender kicks the ball out-of-bounds, then neither player gets a point.

-To make the drill easier for attackers, widen the field. To make the drill easier for defenders, make the field narrower.

-Consider 1v2s, 2v1s, & 2v2s.

# Chapter 17

# Defending Drill 3—Forcing the Attacker

**# of Players Needed:** 2-8 per grid

**Purpose:**

-To work on 1v1s and develop attacking and defending players' skills.

-To teach defenders how to push attacking players in the direction that the defender wants them to travel.

-To develop speed when closing down an attacker.

**Setup:**

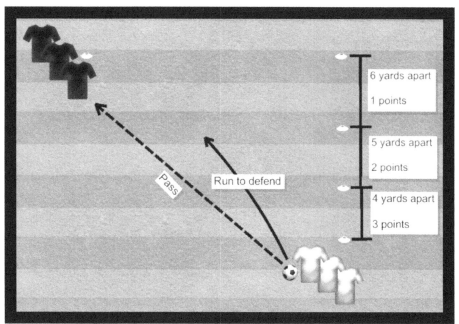

1. In each grid, divide the players into two teams. One team will attack first, while the other defends.

2. With four cones, make three gates in a line.

3. Gate 1 should be six yards wide. An attacking player who dribbles the ball through this gate earns one point.

4. Gate 2 should be five yards wide. An attacking player who dribbles the ball through this gate earns two points.

5. Make Gate 3 four yards wide. An attacking player who dribbles the ball through this gate earns three points.

6. Have the defending players start at the last cone of the Gate 3, with two soccer balls each.

7. Place one cone 20 yards away from the first cone of Gate 1. Start the attacking players at this cone, with no soccer balls.

**How to Play:**

1. The first defender starts by passing to the first attacker.

2. Once the defender passes the ball, they sprint towards the attacker.

3. The attacker takes a moving first touch and dribbles towards the gates.

4. The attacker attempts to score on each turn.

5. The defender attempts to: (1) direct the attacker towards Gate 1; (2) kick the ball away; or (3) dispossess the attacking player entirely.

6. Once the attacker dribbles through a gate, or the defender wins the ball, the next two players can begin their turn.

7. Only award points for players who dribble through the gate while maintaining possession. Do not award points to attacking players who just kick the ball through the gate.

8. The coach, a trustworthy player, or both teams should keep track of the points scored by the attackers each round.

## Sets:

-Have 1 round last 7 minutes; 3 minutes for the first attacking team to attack, 1 minute to collect soccer balls and switch sides, and then another 3 minutes for the defending team to become attackers.

-Play 3 total rounds. The team that scores higher in at least 2 rounds wins.

## Coaching Points:

1. Give players a "free" round to figure out the drill for themselves, which will help them develop their problem-solving abilities. Then, consider giving hints after each set.

2. Explain the importance of channeling an attacker in a real game: 1) force them out-of-bounds; 2) force them to their opposite foot; and 3) force them towards another defender.

3. A great defender determines where the attacker goes.

4. Defenders should aim to get close enough to the attackers so the attacker will put their head down and lose vision of the field.

Better attackers will keep their heads up for longer, while lesser players will be quick to put their heads down.

**Variations:**

-If a defender wins the ball from the attacker, then they can score in any of the gates. This will develop an attacking player's mindset to recover quickly when they lose the ball and attempt to win it back in the critical six-second window after the ball is lost.

-Make the gates smaller or larger.

-Change the scoring system to one point for the largest gate, three points for the middle gate, and six points for the smallest gate.

-Move the attacking player's cone closer to or farther away from the gates.

# Chapter 18

# *Defending Drill 4—1v1 No Turn*

**# of Players Needed:** 3-9 per grid

**Purpose:**

-To work on 1v1s with the attacker's back turned to goal.

-To develop a defender's ability to keep an attacker from turning with the ball.

-Defenders improve their aggressiveness, strength, and placing a forearm on the defender.

-Attackers become better with their back facing goal while developing their ability to hold a ball, turn, and shoot.

**Setup:**

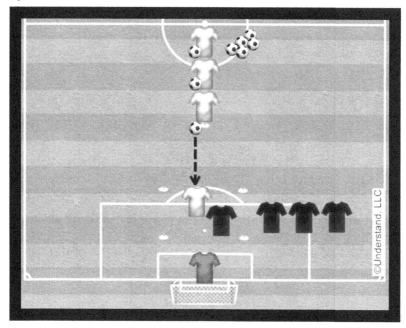

1. Use one goalkeeper to make this drill more game-like.

2. If no goalkeepers are available, then use two cones to help represent scoring near either post. Place the cones one yard towards the inside of the goal. Shots between either post and the nearest cone, will count as a goal.

3. Create a 20 X 20-yard box in front of the goal. The box should start eight yards away from the goal.

4. Split the field players between the attacking lines and the defending lines, as shown in the image. Set up the soccer balls at the attacking line. If there are assigned positions on your team, then have the defenders defend the entire time, and the offensive players work with their backs facing the goal.

5. Have one attacker and one defender start inside the 20 X 20-yard box. The rest of the players should form a line 10 yards with all the soccer balls behind the box.

6. If you have over eight players, then make multiple grids. If you do not have additional goals for extra grids, then require the attacker to shoot/pass/dribble the ball into a small, portable goal or through a gate that is two yards wide.


**How to Play:**

1. The first player in line starts by playing a ball into the attacking player's feet.

2. The attacker receives the ball with their back to goal while the defender applies pressure on their backside. The defender can even attempt to steal the ball as it is played to the attacker.

3. The attacker attempts to turn and score on the defender while staying inside the box.

4. The defender attempts to intercept the ball, dispossess the attacker, block the attacker's shot, or force the attacker outside of the box.

5. 2 points are awarded to the defender who prevents the attacker from turning.

6. 1 point is awarded to the defender who allows the attacker to turn with the ball but does not score.

7. 0 points are awarded to the defender if the attacker turns and scores.

8. The turn is finished when the attacker scores, loses the ball, or is forced out of the box.

9. Once the ball is dispossessed or shot, one player from each line enters the square and the next set begins.

**Sets:**

-Perform 4 rounds lasting 5 minutes each.

**Coaching Points:**
1. Reveal that the box has been set up for the defenders because, in an actual game, if they can push the attacker outside the box, then a supporting defender will probably be there to help. Forcing an attacking player towards a teammate is almost always a good thing to do.

2. A defender should be patient when the attacker is dribbling towards them with the ball. However, in this drill, defenders should be aggressive when the attacker's back is facing where they need to score.

3. Remind the defenders to get tight enough to the attacker so that they cannot turn but not so close that the attacker rolls off their forearm and turns.

4. Defenders should not be front-facing (or "squared") to the attacker. Have them facing the attacker side-on, with a forearm placed against their arm or backside.

5. Emphasize that the attackers need to check to the ball or risk the defender intercepting the pass.

6. Teach the attackers to pick a move to turn with, commit to it, and be explosive when turning.

**Variations:**

-Instead of having attacker and defender lines, have the passer become the attacker in the next set, have the attacker become the defender, and have the defender grab the soccer ball before traveling back into the line.

-Change the location of the 20 X 20-yard box. Move the box closer to the goal to make it easier for attackers or move it farther from the goal to make it easier for defenders and the goalkeeper.

-Move the 20 X 20-yard box farther to the left or right to create different attacking and defending angles.

-Increase the 20 X 20-yard box's size to make it easier for forwards or decrease the box's size to make it easier for defenders and the goalkeeper.

-Remove the box entirely, resulting in a turn that only ends when the defender dispossesses the attacker or the attacker shoots.

-Instead of a pass on the ground, make a pass to the forward by lofting the ball in the air.

**YouTube:** If you would like to see a video on this defending drill, then consider watching the *Understand Soccer* YouTube video: *Soccer 1v1 Defending Drills*.

# Shooting Drills

# Chapter 19

# Shooting Drill 1—Shooting with Both Feet

**# of Players Needed:** 9-22

**Purpose:**

-To develop your team's build-up, play to move the ball towards the other team's net.

-To practice two of the Big 3 skills.

-To work on exploding with speed after a skill.

-To improve shooting power and accuracy.

**Setup:**

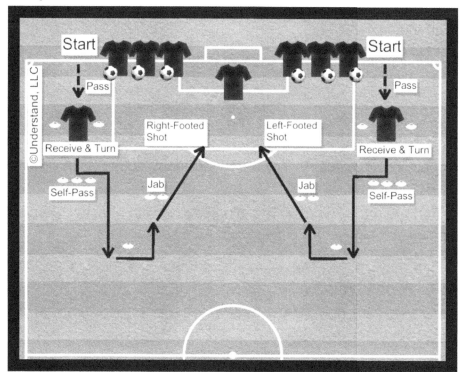

1. Two starting lines instead of one means there are twice as many shots being taken. Twice as many shots results in quicker improvement for your players, and increased reaction time for your goalkeeper.

2. Begin at the "Start" and pass to a player eight yards away.

3. The receiving player should turn and attack the three cones in a line.

4. Do a self-pass/la croqueta from your right to your left foot (or vice versa.)

5. Accelerate past the cone nearest the halfway line. Use a chop turn just past the cone.

6. Attack the two cones and perform a right/left-footed jab step.

7. Take a big push past the cones and accelerate to the ball.

8. The left side shoots right-footed, and the right side shoots left-footed.

9. Players should switch lines after they shoot.


**Sets:**

-Aim to have the players work to score a certain amount of goals in 4 minutes. If they meet your goal, up the score to beat for the next round.

-Perform 4 total sets each 4 minutes long with a minute break in between each set for players to collect soccer balls.


**Coaching Points:**

1. Have your players use only one push to accelerate to the next set of cones.

2. Players should dribble with their heads slightly up, not straight down looking at the ball.

3. Make sure the person receiving the ball is yelling and demanding the ball.

4. Make sure the players know that though the most fun part of the drill may be shooting, the most important parts are the passing and dribbling leading up to the shot. If your team cannot move the ball up the field, they will never have the opportunity to shoot.

5. This drill is included in the free PDF printout at UnderstandSoccer.com/free-printout. This drill is an excerpt from the *Understand Soccer* series book, *Soccer Coaching*.

## Variations:

-You can have players perform a roll instead of self-pass and a scissor instead of jab step (body feint). However, these are slower skills to use in these situations, so it is not recommended.

-Instead of scoring a certain amount of goals in 4 minutes, have players perform 3 laps (i.e., 6 shots per player) and see who can score the most goals.

# Chapter 20

## Shooting Drill 2—Shooters' Paradise

**# of Players Needed:** 8-20

**Purpose:**

-To train your team to think more about shooting constantly, given that the team with more shots is often victorious.

-To develop your attacking players' quick reactions in the 18-yard box.

-To enhance your defending players' ability to close space, stay close to attacking players, and block shots.

-To improve your players' ability to make and receive passes in tight spaces.

**Setup:**

1. Using the 44-yard width of the 18-yard box, set cones down to create a playing field that is 30 yards long.

2. Set up nets on both sides of the field.

3. Ideally, two players should be designated goalkeepers for the entire game.

4. The number of players you have in your practice will determine how you split up the teams. Use bibs/pennies for this drill if you have them. Otherwise, split players by their shirt color.

| # of Players | Team Size |
|---|---|
| 8 players | 3v3 & 2 all-time goalkeepers |
| 10 players | 4v4 & 2 all-time goalkeepers |
| 12 players | 5v5 & 2 all-time goalkeepers |
| 14 players | 3 teams of 4 players & 2 all-time goalkeepers |
| 17 players | 3 teams of 5 players & 2 all-time goalkeepers |
| 20 players | 3 teams of 6 players & 2 all-time goalkeepers |

5. Two teams start on the field. Any additional teams will be off to the side and should collect soccer balls.

6. Keep the soccer balls near the goal or inside it, so the goalkeeper can resume play quickly.

7. If the ball goes out-of-bounds, then the goalkeeper of the team that did not have the last touch will start a new ball.

8. If a team scores, then the goalkeeper who was scored on will start a new ball. Do not allow goalkeepers to shoot, as this is not a necessary skill for them to develop.

## Sets:

-Play 3 to 5-minute games. Each team should play at least twice.

-Award teams 3 points for a win, 1 point for a draw, and 0 points for a loss.

## Coaching Points:

1. Reveal to the players that a goal can be scored at any moment. Therefore, they need to be paying attention constantly.

2. Challenge the defending team to immediately close the space of the other team to prevent shots.

3. Emphasize the importance of taking a shot when a player has it. After all, this drill is about your players in the mindset of once they are near the goal, they should look to shoot.

4. Remind your players that they only need a foot of space for the ball to travel past the defender. Too many players look to have more than a yard of space to consider shooting.

## Variations:

-Limit players' touches to three or two touches.

-Instead of making it so each team plays the same amount of games, provide an incentive to win by allowing the team that scores first to stay on. The team that concedes a goal must immediately go off the field.

-Instead of scoring each game, have the cumulative goals scored across every game for a team count as their final score.

-If there are more than two teams, have the team that is off positioned along the two sidelines. The attacking team can use these players to set up play by passing the ball to them.

# Chapter 21

## Shooting Drill 3—One-Touch Shooting

**# of Players Needed:** 9-22

**Purpose:**

-To improve one-touch passing skills.
-To practice two-and-one-touch finishing.

**Setup:**

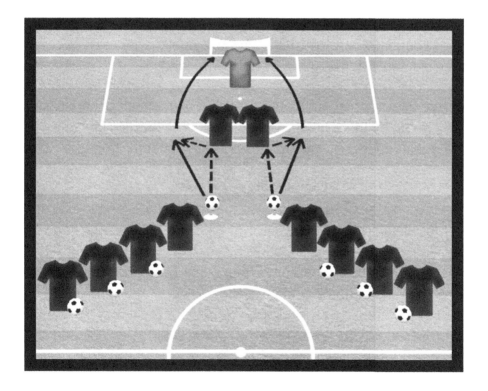

1. Have players form two lines about 8-12 yards outside the 18-yard box.

2. Each player in line should have a soccer ball.

3. Designate two players on your team as passers. Assign players who typically pass frequently to these spots. For example, designate two defensive center midfielders to lay the balls off for other players to shoot. Also, consider rotating the passing player after each set.

4. Have a goalkeeper in the goal. If there are extra goalkeepers, then have them rotate every four shots.

5. Start both lines at the same time, knowing that the lines will soon become out of sync, so the goalkeeper will not see multiple shots at the same time for very long.

6. Avoid letting players attempt to score rebounds, because they may be hit by the next shooter and become hurt, or they may hit the goalkeeper, who will be looking at the shooter from the other line.

7. Have players recover their shots if they are wide, over the net, or blocked by the keeper. For example, I will often stand by the passers to tell the shooting players what to improve in their shooting form or by the net to help place balls back into the line to ensure a smooth flow to the drill.

8. After shooting, have players rotate lines. The left line will shoot left-footed, and the right line will shoot right-footed.

## Sets:

-Perform 3-4 sets with each lasting 4-5 minutes.

## Coaching Points:

1. Teach players the difference between a pass shot and driven shot. Generally, use pass shots when one-timing the ball or shooting no farther than the penalty spot. Tell players to use driven shots when farther from the net than the penalty spot and not a one-touch shot.

2. Emphasize that players strike the ball low into the corners of the goal instead of just attempting to hit the soccer ball as hard as possible with little concern for accuracy.

3. Instruct players to keep their head and chest over the ball to avoid shooting the ball too high. Also, instruct players to not watch their shots because it compromises form.

4. Have players follow through the ball when shooting. They should be shooting using the momentum of their entire body, not just their leg. Also, following through the ball makes it easier to get rebounds in an actual game.

5. Coach players to target a specific spot in net when shooting. Do not shoot to shoot. Shoot to score.

## Variations:

-Depending on the abilities of your players, consider requiring players to shoot with their first touch.

-Move the players laying off the ball closer to the net to emphasize shooters placing the ball with the inside of their foot.

-Move the players laying off the ball farther from the net to emphasize shooters striking the ball with their toe down and out using the bone of their foot.

-Have players laying of the pass loft the ball so shooters must strike the ball as a half-volley or full volley.

# Chapter 22

## Shooting Drill 4—Two-Sided Goal

**# of Players Needed:** 6-10

**Purpose:**

-To work on different striking forms.

-To emphasize following through after the shot to increase shot power.

-To practice striking with their opposite foot.

**Setup:**

1. Place two cones 15 yards apart. These will act as the goal.

2. On one side of the goal, create a line using two cones that are five yards apart. These will be a team's side to shoot from.

3. Create another line using two cones that are five yards apart on the other side of the goal. These will be the second team's side to shoot from.

4. To create the lines on the opposite sides of the goal, you must first determine the ages of your players, as well as how skilled they are at shooting. See the below chart for reference:

| Player Age | Space Between Cones |
|---|---|
| 6 and under | 10 yards |
| 7-9 years old | 12 yards |
| 10-12 years old | 15 yards |
| 13+ years old | 18 yards |

**How to Play:**

1. One team will start with a player in the net. This player can use their hands to save a shot.

2. The first player in line on the opposite team will strike a shot.

3. Since there are only cones and not an actual net, tell your players that a goal must be at the goalkeeper's head-height or lower. This takes the height advantage away from taller players.

4. After shooting, the player has three seconds to travel into the net to stop the opposing player's shot.

5. The goalkeeper grabs the ball that was shot at them and travels back to their team's line.

6. Do not allow players to shoot rebounds.

7. Each team takes alternating shots on the goal.

8. For each competing team, the team with the most goals at the end of the round wins.

## Sets:

-Play 4 rounds each 4 minutes long with a minute break in between each set. Rotate teams so each team plays a different opponent each round.

## Coaching Points:

1. Emphasize placement and power, with more importance on placement.

2. Remind players to be constantly asking, "What should I do and where should I be next." In this drill, if a player is not thinking, they will forget to travel into the goal and allow for an easy point to the other team.

## Variations:

-Different ways to strike the ball for each round:

1. Driven Shot
2. Bent Shot
3. Pass Shot
4. Outside-of-the-Foot Shot

-Additional rounds could involve half-volleys and full volleys, in which a teammate tosses the ball to the striking player. Both players stay behind the line formed by the two cones.

**YouTube:** If you would like to see a video on this shooting drill, then consider watching the *Understand Soccer* YouTube video: *Soccer Small Sided Games Shooting*.

# *Chapter 23*

# *Games*

In this chapter, we will discuss several fun soccer games. These are many of my soccer players' favorites and can be used as an incentive to ensure that players are paying attention and working hard throughout the practice.

The games covered in this chapter are:

1. World Cup

2. Lightning

3. Soccer Dodgeball

4. Sharks & Minnows

5. Knockout

# Chapter 24

## Game 1—World Cup

1. Divide players into teams of either two or three players.

2. Have a coach or the team's goalkeeper be the goalkeeper for the game. They will also be tasked with throwing balls into play when they go out-of-bounds.

3. Have each team pick a country/club/funny team name for themselves.

4. Use half the field, with all the teams on the field to start.

5. The coach will throw the ball into the middle of the playing area.

6. The maximum recommended number of balls you can use is one less than the number of teams on the field. So, if you have three teams, then you can use a maximum of two balls.

7. With more than one active ball, it will become dangerous if players are not paying attention to the ball being shot on goal. If you elect to use more than one ball, then make sure to be vocal when players shoot and warn everyone to pay attention.

8. A team's objective is to score on the goalkeeper, while preventing the other teams from scoring first.

9. Saved shots can be thrown back into play by the goalkeeper.

10. Designate the six-yard box as a "no-shot zone," where players cannot score.

11. Once a team scores, they can go behind the goal to relax until the next round. As the coach, you can also ask them to collect soccer balls, so the remaining teams on the field will not have to waste time looking for them.

12. Deflections count for the team that shot the ball, but a redirection of the ball counts for the team that redirected the path of the ball significantly enough to cause it to go into the goal.

13. The team that did not score in that round is eliminated. All the other teams that scored will go back onto the field for the next round.

14. Play multiple rounds to eliminate all but two teams. Those two teams will then compete in the "World Cup Final."

15. The team that scores first wins!

**Coaching Points:**

1. Emphasize teamwork. It does not matter who scores on a team, as long as someone does. Therefore, look for passes which will allow teammates easier opportunities to score.

2. Instruct players to practice their "Big 3" foot skills: jab step (body feint), self-pass, and shot fake. (If you are interested in learning how to perform these skills, then grab a copy of the *Understand Soccer* series book, *Soccer Dribbling & Foot Skills*.

**Variations:**

-If you have a lot of players, then you can pick two goalkeepers in two separate goals on opposite sides of half the field.

-Players must call their team name when shooting if they want the goal to count, which will force players to think more while playing.

-If a player from a team that is out catches a missed shot to the side or over top of the goal, then their team is back in the game. This makes it more engaging because a team must remain aware for a chance to catch a ball and get back in the game. However, the two final teams are locked. Remember, this variation takes much more time, so it is better used during camps.

-In the final game, the team who scores two goals first wins.

# Chapter 25

# Game 2—Lightning

Another favorite of soccer players, this game is better to play when you have multiple goals to use. Having a team of players take one shot at a time on goal is not a recipe for a great practice, as too many players will be waiting idly for their turn.

1. One player starts in the goal. Whether or not they are scored on, they grab the ball and travel to the back of the line after their turn in the goal.

2. The first player in line has their ball set on the penalty spot.

3. After the shot is taken, they immediately run into the goal to become the next goalkeeper.

4. The next player can shoot after two full seconds.

5. If the shooter scores they are safe, even if they let in a goal as goalkeeper.

6. If the shooter misses their shot, they must save the next shot to stay in the game or hope it goes wide or over the goal.

7. If the shooter misses and they are scored on, then they are out.

8. The last player remaining is the winner.


**Coaching Points:**

1. Observe the goalkeeper's position.

2. Players must keep their head down and chest over the ball when shooting.

3. Players should use either a pass shot or driven shot when shooting.


**Variations:**

-Players must shoot from outside the 18-yard box.

-The player's ball must be rolling when they shoot behind a certain point/line on the field.

-Any previously out players who catch wide shots or shots over the goal are back in the game.

# Chapter 26

## Game 3—Soccer Dodgeball

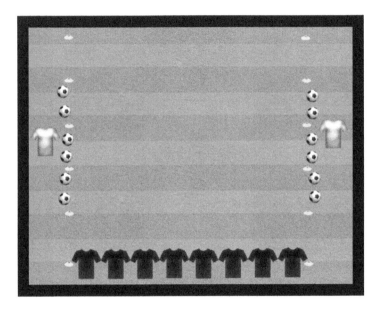

1. Set up a grid 20 yards wide X 30 yards long. Split all soccer balls between the two 30-yards-long sides.

2. Two players/coaches will start with one additional player or coach on each side of the field, who will have possession of the balls.

3. In each round, players will run from one end of the rectangle to the other, while the players/coaches on the outside will attempt to hit them below the knees with a ball.

4. If a player is hit with a ball, then they are out and must go to one of the sides to take possession of the balls. In subsequent rounds, they will help strike balls to get more players out.

5. Keep playing more rounds until only one player is left who has not been hit by a ball.

6. Between each round, the remaining players should wait for the players who are out to collect the balls that will be used in the next round.

7. After you say, "Go," to begin each round, players will have five seconds to start running from one side of the field to the other.

8. Require shots to be knee-height or lower. Give only one warning to players who kick it too high and attempt to injure a player. If they are caught kicking the ball too high for a second time, then they are banned from the game.

9. If a player is hit higher than their knees with the ball, then they are still in the game. No cheating!

## Coaching Points:

1. Emphasize the form for a driven shot or pass shot. If you are interested in learning the steps for these different forms, grab a copy of the *Understand Soccer* series book, *Soccer Shooting & Finishing*.

2. Recommend players to keep scanning to see when balls are coming towards them.

## Variations:

-Widen or narrow the field depending on the age of your players.

-Play so that players who are out can only strike the ball using their opposite foot.

# Chapter 27

## Game 4—Sharks & Minnows

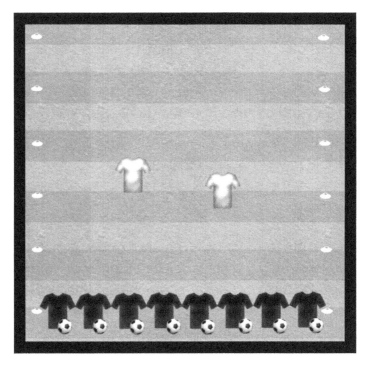

1. Set up a 20 X 30-yard grid.

2. Players start on one of the 20-yard sides of the grid.

3. Players are called "minnows." Each one gets a soccer ball.

4. There are two "sharks" who can be players or coaches. They will start in the middle of the grid, without a ball.

5. During each round, every minnow must dribble the ball from one 20-yard sideline to the other.

6. In each round, the sharks must attempt to kick the minnows' balls out of the grid as the minnows dribble the balls from one side to the other.

7. Minnows with balls kicked out of the grid will become sharks in subsequent rounds.

8. The last two minnows who have not been eliminated are allowed take the place of the sharks for the next round.

9. You can let them become minnows again if they do not want to be a shark. Select another player to fill their spot as a shark instead.

**Coaching Points:**

1. When players are dribbling, emphasize that they should keep their toes down and slightly in when they push the ball.

2. Show players the difference between speed dribbling (i.e., taking a touch every step to have the ball close to them at all times) and dribbling at speed (i.e., taking larger touches when no defenders are near them to travel farther in less time versus taking smaller touches when defenders are near them to keep control of the ball and react quickly if the defender reaches in for the ball).

**Variations:**

-For each new game, let the winning minnows from the last round choose what animal they want to be that round instead of sharks and what animal they want the minnows to be called.

-Require minnows to only dribble with their opposite foot.

# Chapter 28

## Game 5—Knockout (aka "King of the Mountain")

1. Make a 15-yard X 15-yard grid.

2. Each player has a ball and must keep it from going outside the grid without using their hands.

3. When you say, "Go," players attempt to kick each other's ball out of the grid, while protecting their own.

4. The game ends when only one player remains in the grid with their ball.

**Coaching Points:**

1. This drill emphasizes a "defense-first" mindset, because players must protect their ball before worrying about kicking the other players' balls out of the grid.

2. Emphasize teamwork by creating alliances.

**Variations:**

-As players get out, have them form a wall on one side of the grid. For each minute that passes, the wall of players should take a step in to decrease the size of the square and give less space to the players remaining.

-Play three rounds. The winners of each round will play in the finals. If one player wins more than once, then that player gets an additional chance in the finals.

# Afterword

The specific drills in this book were included to help each player on your team improve in key areas. Feel free to change the drills and adapt them as you see fit based on your team's skills and abilities, while attempting to bring as much fun and enjoyment to your practices as you can.

Remember not to think of this book as something that should never be picked back up. **Instead, after reading it through the first time, you can use it as a reference for upcoming practices or future seasons.** Pictures have been included for most of the drills, so you can quickly flip back through the book for some refreshers and ideas for practices.

To be a great coach, you must continue learning, growing, and always working to find what works best for you and your team. Johan Cruyff, the famous soccer star and coach, said towards the end of his career that, "*I still have a lot of room for improvement.*" Therefore, learn from his wisdom and do not stop improving your soccer knowledge as there is a considerable amount for every coach, trainer, parent, and player to learn. You have taken the time to read this book, so you have already revealed that you likely care more and are more committed than most other coaches. Therefore, I applaud you for your efforts and want to let you know they have not gone unnoticed.

**If you have enjoyed this book, please leave a review on Amazon to let me know.** If you are interested in the exact form for many of the player-specific skills (e.g., which shots are best in each situation; exactly how to perform the "Big 3" foot skills; how to create more time in a game for some of your players who are not as confident with the ball; how a defender should act based on what the opposing attacking player is doing), then grab other books in the *Understand Soccer* series to continue advancing your knowledge of this "beautiful game!"

# WAIT!

Wouldn't it be nice to have an easy two-page FREE PDF printout with two already-made practice plans? Well, here is your chance!

Go to this Link for an **Instant** Two-Page Printout:
UnderstandSoccer.com/free-printout

These two FREE practice plans are simply a thank you for purchasing this book. These PDF printouts will ensure that you have terrific practices for your soccer team!

# About the Author

There he was—a soccer player who had difficulties scoring. He wanted to be the best on the field but lacked the confidence and knowledge to make his goal a reality. Every day, he dreamed about improving, but the average coaching he received, combined with his lack of knowledge, only left him feeling alone and unable to attain his goal. He was a quiet player, and his performance often went unnoticed.

This all changed after his junior year on the varsity soccer team of one of the largest high schools in the state. During the team and parent banquet at the end of the season, his coach decided to say something nice about each player. When it was his turn to receive praise, the only thing that could be said was that he had scored two goals that season—even though they were against a lousy team, so they didn't really count. It was a very painful statement that after the 20+ game season, all that could be said of his efforts were two goals that didn't count. One of his greatest fears came true; he was called out in front of his family and friends.

Since that moment, he was forever changed. He got serious. With a new soccer mentor, he focused on training to obtain the necessary skills, build his confidence, and become the goal-scorer that he'd always dreamed of being. The next season, after just a few months, he found himself moved up to the starting position of center midfielder and scored his first goal of the 26-game season in only the third game.

He continued with additional training led by a proven goal-scorer to build his knowledge. Fast-forward to the present day, and, as a result of the work he put in, and his focus on the necessary skills, he figured out how to become a goal-scorer who averages about two goals and an assist per game—all because he increased his understanding of how to play soccer. With the help of a soccer mentor, he took his game from being a bench-warmer who got called out in front of everybody to becoming the most confident player on the field.

Currently, he is a soccer trainer in Michigan, working for Next Level Training. He advanced through their rigorous program as a soccer player and was hired as a trainer. This program has allowed him to guide world-class soccer players for over a decade. He trains soccer players in formats ranging from one-hour classes to weeklong camps, and he instructs classes of all sizes, from groups of 30 soccer players all the way down to working one-on-one with individuals who want to play for the United States National Team.

If you enjoyed this book, then please leave a review.

**Additional Books by Dylan Joseph Available on Amazon:**

Soccer Shooting & Finishing: A Step-by-Step Guide on How to Score

Soccer Dribbling & Foot Skills: A Step-by-Step Guide on How to Dribble Past the Other Team

Soccer Defending: A Step-by-Step Guide on How to Stop the Other Team

Soccer Coaching: A Step-by-Step Guide on How to Lead Your Players, Manage Parents, and Select the Best Formation

# Free Book!

How would you like to get a book of your choosing in the *Understand Soccer* series for free?

Join the Soccer Squad Book Team today and receive your next book (and potentially future books) for FREE.

Signing up is easy and does not cost anything.

Check out this website for more information:

UnderstandSoccer.com/soccer-squad-book-team

# Thank You for Reading!

Dear Reader,

I hope you enjoyed and learned from **Soccer Drills**. I truly enjoyed writing these drills to ensure that you and your team have great practices.

As an author, I love feedback. Candidly, you are the reason that I wrote this book and plan to write more. Therefore, tell me what you liked, what you loved, and what can be improved. I would love to hear from you. Visit UnderstandSoccer.com and scroll to the bottom of the homepage to leave me a message in the contact section or email me at:

Dylan@UnderstandSoccer.com

Finally, I need to ask a favor. **I would love and truly appreciate a review.**

As you likely know, reviews are a key part of my process to see whether you, the reader, enjoyed my book. Reviews allow me to write more books. You have the power to help make or break my book. Please take two minutes to leave a review on Amazon.com at: https://www.amazon.com/gp/product-review/1949511278.

In gratitude,

- 119 -

# Glossary

**10 & 4** - The defensive position in which your feet represent the hands on a clock. Use this position when you want to push the attacking player to their left foot.

**8 & 2** - The defensive position in which your feet represent hands on a clock. Use this position when you want to push the attacking player to their right foot.

**80/20 Principle** - 80% of your results come from only 20% of your actions.

**Bent/Curved Shot** - A shot that spins and curves as it goes towards the net. This shot is used when you need to shoot around defenders or goalkeepers. Though you use the bone of your foot to strike the ball instead of following through the ball with your entire body, you just follow through with your leg and cross your legs after shooting the ball.

**Bicycle Kick (i.e., "Overhead Kick")** - where the ball is above you and you jump up and kick the ball over your body while the ball is in the air.

**Big 3 Foot Skills** - The jab step (body feint), the self-pass, and the shot fake.

**Block** - Deflecting or stopping the shot of an opposing player.

**Chop** - This is performed with the outside of your foot. The leg that is cutting the ball must step entirely past the ball. Then, allow the ball to hit that leg/foot, which effectively stops the ball. Having the ball stop next to your foot enables the ball to be pushed in a different direction quickly.

**Cruyff** - Cut the ball but leave yourself between it and the defender. In essence, you are cutting the ball behind your plant leg.

**Cut** - This is performed with the inside of your foot. The leg that is cutting the ball must step entirely past the ball. Then, allow the ball to hit that leg/foot, which will effectively stop the ball. Stopping the ball next to your foot will enable it to be pushed in a different direction quickly. Additionally, you may cut the ball so it will be immediately moving in the direction you want to go.

**Driven Shot** - A shot struck with the bone of your foot, where you follow through with your entire body without crossing your legs. This is the most powerful type of shot.

**Finishing** - The purpose of shooting which is to score.

**Half-Volley** - Striking the ball just after it hit the ground, but while the ball is still in the air.

**Jab Step (i.e., "Feint," "Body Feint," "Fake," "Fake and Take," or "Shoulder Drop")** - When you pretend to push the ball in one direction, but purposely miss, then plant with the foot that you missed the ball with to push the ball in the other direction.

**Jockeying** - When defending, backpedaling to maintain a proper position in relation to the person attacking with the ball. When jockeying, the defender does not dive in for the ball. They wait for the ideal time to steal the ball or poke it away instead.

**Jog-Through Lap** - When performing a drill, these are the 1-2 laps that you allow your players to walk/jog-through at the beginning to make sure they understand what to do and ask questions.

**Jump Turn** - Instead of pulling the ball back with the bottom of your foot, as you would do in the V pull-back, you will stop the ball with the bottom of your foot as you jump past it, then land with both feet on the other side of the ball at the same time. This will allow you to explode away in the direction from which you came.

**Moving First Touch (i.e., "Attacking Touch")** - Pushing the ball into space with your first touch, which is the opposite of taking a touch where the ball stops underneath you (i.e., at your feet).

**Offside** - When you pass the ball to a player on your team who is past the opposing team's last defender at the moment the kick is initiated. You cannot be offside on a throw-in or when you are on your own half of the field.

**Opposite Foot** - Your non-dominant foot. Out of your two feet, it is the one you are not as comfortable using.

**Practice Plan** - A 1-page summary of the drills that you want to perform during your team's practice. Often this plan will have coaching points to remind you what to teach during each drill.

**Roll (i.e., "Rollover")** - Using the bottom of the toes of your foot, roll the ball parallel to the defender, crossing your feet when you plant. Then, bring your other foot around to uncross your feet and push the ball forward. The path the ball takes is the shape of an "L."

**Rondo** - A training game similar to "keep away" where one group of players must maintain possession of the ball by passing it around members of the opposing side.

**Sandwich Feedback Technique** - Give a compliment, followed by giving feedback with an explanation ended with another compliment.

**Scissor** - When the foot closest to the ball goes around the ball as you are attacking in a game. Emphasize turning your hips to fake the defender. To easily turn your hips, plant past the ball with your foot that is not going around the ball so that you can use the momentum of the moving ball to your advantage.

**Self-Pass (i.e., "L," "Iniesta," or "La Croqueta")** - Passing the ball from one foot to the other while running. Imagine you are doing a roll, but without your foot going on top of the ball. Instead, it is an inside of the foot pass from one foot and an inside of the foot push up the field with the other foot.

**Shot Fake** - Faking a shot. Make sure your form looks the same as when you shoot, including: 1) Looking at the goal before you do a shot fake 2) Arms out 3) Raise your shooting leg high enough behind your body, so it looks like you will shoot.

**Small-Sided Scrimmages** - Scrimmages where each team has no more than five players. These types of scrimmages are better than full-field scrimmages because more players will be touching the ball at any one time thereby increasing players skills with the ball and confidence more quickly.

**Step-On-Step-Out** - To change direction, step on the ball with the bottom of your foot. Then, with the same foot that stepped on the ball, take another step to plant to the side of the ball so that your other leg can come through and push the ball in a different direction.

**Step-Over** - When you are next to the ball, step over the ball with the leg farthest away from it, so your entire body will turn as if you were going in a completely different direction. The step-over is best used along a sideline.

**V Pull-Back** - Pull the ball backward using the bottom of your foot. Then, use your other leg to push the ball and accelerate forward in the other direction (hence the "V" in the V pull-back.)

**Volley** - Striking the ball out of the air before it hits the ground.

**Wall Passing (i.e., "1-2 Passing")** - A wall pass is when you pass it to a teammate, and they pass it back to you with one touch, similar to if you were to pass a ball against a wall.

# Acknowledgments

First, I would like to thank you, the reader. I am grateful to provide you with value and help you on your journey of coaching and developing young players. I am happy to serve you, and I thank you for the opportunity to do so.

Also, I would like to recognize people who have made a difference and paved the way for me to share this book with you:

I want to thank the grammar editor Abbey Decker. Her terrific understanding of the complexities of the English language ensured that the wording needed to convey the messages was appropriate, and she provided countless grammatical improvements.

Also, I would like to thank the content editors: Kevin Solorio, Toni Sinistaj, and Youssef Hodroj. They reviewed this book for areas that could be improved, and additional insights to share with you, the reader.

Many thanks,

*Dylan Joseph*

Made in the USA
Monee, IL
01 March 2022

92060122R10075